BEST EVER

CHOCOLATE

CAKES & SLICES

A selection of temptations that no
chocoholic will be able to resist.

MURDOCH BOOKS

Sydney • London

Cake tins

There are many shapes and sizes of tin from which to choose. Buy yourself a good range so that you can make all manner of cakes. The shape of some tins – one with fluted sides, for example – greatly enhances the look of the finished product.

If you want to substitute one tin for another, measure the volume of the batter and pour the same amount of water into the tin you intend to use. As long as the water does not come any higher than two-thirds up the tin, you can use it. As a general rule, a cake tin should be half full, and never more than two-thirds full of batter, unless the recipe states otherwise.

1 Deep round cake tin 28 cm. 2 Recess flan tin 23 cm. 3 Deep round cake tin 20 cm. 4 Ring tin 20 cm. 5 Loaf tin 25 x 15 x 5.5 cm. 6 Loaf tin 21 x 14 x 7 cm. 7 Long bar tin 26 x 8 x 4.5 cm. 8 Shallow oblong tin 30 x 20 cm. 9 Shallow Swiss roll tin 30 x 25 x 2 cm. 10 Deep patty tin 12 cup. 11 Shallow patty tin 12 cup. 12 Shallow round cake tin 20 cm. 13 Round springform tin 20 cm . 14 Baba tin 20 cm. 15 Deep square cake tin 19 cm.

1. Lining a square tin. On greaseproof paper, trace square and cut it out.

2. Use a pastry brush to grease the base and sides of the tin with melted butter.

3. Place the square of greaseproof paper in the base of the greased tin.

1. Lining a round tin.
Trace a circle onto a sheet
of greaseproof paper.

2. Cut two strips for side.
Make 2 cm long diagonal
cuts down one side of each.

3. Grease tin. Press strips
cut side down around side
of tin. Press circle over base.

Cake decorations

Chocolate decorations such as leaves and silhouettes give your cake making a truly professional look. Fruit dipped in chocolate is also a simple after-dinner treat. Melt the chocolate carefully before use.

Melting Chocolate

Break chocolate into small pieces and place in a glass bowl. Set the bowl over barely simmering water and stir chocolate gently until melted. Do not allow a drop of water to fall on the chocolate or it will stiffen dramatically and be unworkable for decoration purposes. Cool slightly before use.

Chocolate Curls

250 g chocolate, chopped

1 Melt chocolate as described above.
2 Pour chocolate onto a marble or Laminex board. Smooth surface lightly.
3 Allow the chocolate to set to room temperature. (It may be necessary to put it in the refrigerator if the weather is humid.)
4 When chocolate has set, use a sharp, flat-bladed knife to make curls.
5 Hold blade at an angle. Apply a constant pressure to blade with both hands. Pull the knife towards you. Varying the pressure on the blade will determine how thick or thin the curls will be.

Dipping Fruit

This method is suitable for petals and for fruit. Hold fresh or dried fruit or petals and dip them into melted chocolate, covering them to the desired degree. Place on a tray lined with baking paper and refrigerate until set.

Coating Leaves

Use clean, non-toxic leaves (rose leaves are good). Brush the melted chocolate onto the underside of the leaf. Place on a tray lined with baking paper and refrigerate until set. Then carefully peel away the leaf.

Silhouettes

You will need a piping bag fitted with a writing tube or a plastic bag. Fill with melted chocolate. If using a plastic bag, then cut off the end. Draw circles,

Vary the pressure on the blade to alter the curl size.

Dip strawberries and rose petals in melted chocolate and leave to set.

Paint leaves with melted chocolate, allow to set, then peel away leaves.

butterflies, stars, squiggles – whatever it is you wish – onto baking paper. Allow to set. Carefully peel away the paper.

Borders

To make chocolate borders to cover the sides of a cake, spread the melted chocolate thickly onto strips of plastic wrap or foil. Mould strips round the sides of a springform tin slightly larger than the cake. Refrigerate. When the chocolate has set,

peel off the plastic wrap or foil. Place chocolate strips around the cake. Alternatively, spread the melted chocolate onto a strip of baking paper the depth and diameter of the cake. Place cake on serving plate. Just before chocolate is set, carefully place the baking paper around the cake. Refrigerate for about 15 minutes. When chocolate has set, carefully peel off paper.

Spiderweb

Ice the cake with white icing and use dark chocolate for the web (or vice versa) to create a striking effect. Leave icing until it is firm. Melt the chocolate for decoration and allow it to cool (it must not start to set as it needs to be workable). Place in a piping bag and pipe concentric circles onto the icing. Draw the point of a skewer or a knife quickly through the circles to produce a feathering effect.

Use a piping bag to 'draw' the shape that you want.

To cover cake sides, spread foil strips with chocolate.

Use point of a skewer to 'feather' melted chocolate.

Family treats

What child doesn't enjoy raiding the cake tin on arriving home hungry from school? And what kind of a Sunday afternoon tea would it be if there were no chocolate sponge to sink your teeth into? The demands of a cake-loving family are hard to meet, but these good looking and great tasting recipes will ensure you're never found wanting. Among them are the ever-popular Chocolate Butterflies, a Mocha Swiss Roll, a stylish Chocolate Pecan Tea Cake and a divine Chocolate and Cherry Layer Cake. Chocolate curls for decoration, smooth icings and fillings turn the simplest recipe into something special.

Easy Chocolate Cake

Preparation time:
  20 minutes
Cooking time:
  35 minutes
Makes 1 x 20 cm round
  cake

125 g butter
3/4 cup caster sugar
1 egg
1 teaspoon imitation
  vanilla essence
1½ cups self-raising
  flour, sifted

1 tablespoon cocoa,
  sifted
½ cup milk
¼ teaspoon
  bicarbonate of soda
¼ cup hot water
½ cup cream, whipped
icing sugar
strawberries

1 Preheat oven to 180°C. Brush two shallow 20 cm round cake tins with melted butter or oil, line base and sides with paper; grease paper.
2 Beat butter and sugar with electric beaters in

From top left: Easy Chocolate Cake,
Marbled Honey and Chocolate Cake (recipe page 9),
White Chocolate and Pear Ring (recipe page 8).

small mixer bowl until light and creamy. Add egg and beat thoroughly. Add essence; beat until combined.

3 Transfer mixture to large mixing bowl. Using a metal spoon, fold in sifted ingredients alternately with milk. Stir until just combined and mixture is almost smooth.

4 Dissolve soda in hot water. Fold into mixture.

5 Spoon mixture into prepared tins; smooth surface. Bake 35 minutes or until skewer comes out clean when inserted in centre of cakes.

6 Stand cakes in tins 5 minutes before turning onto wire rack to cool.

7 Sandwich cakes together with whipped cream. Dust with icing sugar and decorate with strawberries.

HINT
You can tell your cake is cooked if the top springs back when you press it lightly with your fingertips. Also, the cake should have come away from the sides of the tin. Always let a cake rest in the tin for a few minutes before you turn it out onto a wire rack to cool.

White Chocolate and Pear Ring

Preparation time:
30 minutes
Cooking time:
40 minutes
Makes 1 x 20 cm ring cake

100 g white chocolate, chopped
125 g butter
1/2 cup caster sugar
2 eggs, separated
1 1/2 cups self-raising flour, sifted
1/2 cup milk
1 x 425 g can pear halves, drained and juice reserved

Icing
reserved pear juice
1/4 cup icing sugar
20 g butter
1-2 teaspoons water

1 Preheat oven to 170°C. Brush a 20 cm ring tin with melted butter or oil. Coat base and side evenly with flour; shake off any excess.

2 Place chocolate in glass bowl. Stir over barely simmering water until melted; remove from heat.

3 Cream butter and sugar with electric beaters in small mixer bowl until light and creamy. Add egg yolks gradually, beating

thoroughly after each addition. Add chocolate, beat until combined.

4 Transfer mixture to large mixing bowl. Using a metal spoon, fold in sifted flour alternately with milk.

5 Place egg whites in a small, clean and dry mixer bowl. Beat until soft peaks form. Using a metal spoon, fold into flour mixture. Stir until just combined and mixture is almost smooth.

6 Spoon half the mixture into prepared tin; slice pears thinly and arrange on top. Spoon remaining mixture over; smooth the surface. Bake 40 minutes or until skewer comes out clean when inserted in the centre of the cake.

7 Stand cake in tin for 6 minutes before turning onto wire rack to cool.

8 To make Icing: Heat pear juice in small pan and simmer, reducing liquid to 1 tablespoon; remove from heat. Stir in icing sugar and butter. Combine with enough water for a thin consistency. Drizzle or pipe over cake.

HINT
All-purpose sugar can be used in place of caster sugar, but it will take a little longer to blend in.

Marbled Honey and Chocolate Cake

Preparation time:
  25 minutes
Cooking time:
  35 minutes
Makes 1 x 20 cm round cake

185 g butter
1/2 cup brown sugar
1/4 cup caster sugar
2 eggs
1 teaspoon imitation
  vanilla essence
1 1/2 cups self-raising
  flour, sifted
2/3 cup milk
1 tablespoon honey
1 tablespoon cocoa,
  sifted
1 tablespoon drinking
  chocolate, sifted

Icing
1 tablespoon honey
2 teaspoons hot water
1/2 cup icing sugar
1 tablespoon cocoa

1 Preheat oven to
180°C. Brush a deep
20 cm (4 cup capacity)
baba tin (see page 2)
with melted butter or
oil. Coat base and side
evenly with flour; shake
off any excess.
2 Beat butter and
sugars with electric
beaters in small mixer
bowl until light and
creamy. Add eggs

gradually, beating
thoroughly after each
addition. Add essence;
beat until combined.
3 Transfer mixture to
large mixing bowl.
Using a metal spoon,
fold in sifted flour
alternately with milk.
Stir until just combined.
4 Divide mixture
evenly between two
bowls. Add honey to
one, and sifted cocoa
and drinking chocolate
to the other; mix well.
5 Spoon the two
mixtures alternately
into prepared tin. Swirl
mixture in circles with
skewer. Bake for
35 minutes or until
skewer comes out clean
when inserted in centre
of cake.
6 Stand cake in tin
10 minutes before
turning onto rack to cool.
7 To make Icing:
Combine honey and
water in small mixing
bowl. Blend in sifted
icing sugar and cocoa;
stir until smooth.
Spread over cake.

Apple Pecan and Chocolate Cake

Preparation time:
  25 minutes
Cooking time:
  45 minutes
Makes a 21 x 14 x 7 cm cake

1 cup self-raising flour,
  sifted
1/2 cup caster sugar
2 tablespoons cocoa,
  sifted
2 eggs, lightly beaten
1/2 cup oil
2 green apples, peeled
  and grated
1/3 cup pecans, chopped
2 teaspoons cocoa, extra
2 tablespoons icing sugar

1 Preheat oven to 180°C.
Brush a 21 x 14 x 7 cm
loaf tin with melted
butter or oil.
Line base with paper;
grease paper.
2 Combine flour, sugar
and cocoa in a medium
mixer bowl.
3 Pour combined eggs
and oil onto dry
ingredients; beat on low
speed for 3 minutes
until just moistened.
4 Beat mixture on high
speed for 5 minutes or
until mixture is free of
lumps and increased in
volume. Using a metal
spoon, fold in the
grated apple and
chopped pecans; stir
until well combined.

9

5 Spoon mixture into prepared tin; smooth surface. Bake 45 minutes or until skewer comes out clean when inserted in centre of cake.

6 Stand cake in tin 10 minutes before turning onto wire rack to cool.

7 Dust cake with combined sifted cocoa and icing sugar, to serve.

Milk Chocolate Cake

Preparation time:
  20 minutes
Cooking time:
  25 minutes
Makes 1 x 23 cm round cake

90 g dark chocolate, chopped
125 g butter
1/2 cup caster sugar
2 eggs, lightly beaten
1/4 cup powdered milk, sifted
1 3/4 cups self-raising flour, sifted
1/2 cup water

Icing
3/4 cup icing sugar, sifted
2 tablespoons powdered milk, sifted
1 tablespoon cocoa, sifted
1 tablespoon hot water
20 g butter, softened

1 Preheat oven to 180°C. Brush a deep 23 cm round cake tin with melted butter or oil, line base and side with paper.

2 Place chocolate in glass bowl. Stir over barely simmering water until melted; remove from heat.

3 Beat butter and sugar with electric beaters in small mixer bowl until light and creamy. Add eggs gradually, beating thoroughly after each addition. Add chocolate; beat until combined.

4 Transfer mixture to large mixing bowl. Using a metal spoon, fold in sifted dry ingredients alternately with water. Stir until just combined and mixture is almost smooth.

5 Spoon mixture into prepared tin; smooth surface. Bake 25 minutes or until skewer comes out clean when inserted in centre of cake.

6 Stand cake in tin 10 minutes before turning onto wire rack to cool.

7 To make Icing: Combine icing sugar, powdered milk and cocoa in small mixing bowl. Blend in water and butter; beat until smooth. Spread evenly over cake using a palette knife.

Apple Pecan and Chocolate Cake (left, recipe page 9), Milk Chocolate Cake.

Mocha Swiss Roll

Preparation time:
  35 minutes
Cooking time:
  8 minutes
Makes 1 Swiss roll

7 *tablespoons plain*
  flour (see Note)
2 *tablespoons cocoa*
2 *teaspoons instant*
  coffee powder
2 *teaspoons baking*
  powder
3 *egg whites*
1/2 *cup caster sugar*
3 *egg yolks, lightly*
  beaten
2 *tablespoons hot milk*
1 *tablespoon caster*
  sugar, extra
1 *cup cream*
1 *teaspoon coffee*
  powder, extra
1 *chocolate bar,*
  crumbled
1/2 *cup flaked almonds*

1 Preheat oven to
220°C. Brush a shallow
30 x 25 x 2 cm Swiss
roll tin with melted
butter or oil. Line base
and two sides with
paper; grease paper.
2 Sift flour, cocoa,
coffee and baking
powder three times
onto greaseproof paper.
3 Place egg whites in
small, clean and dry
mixer bowl. Beat until
soft peaks form.
4 Add sugar gradually,
beating constantly until
mixture is glossy and
thick and all the sugar
is dissolved.
5 Add the beaten egg
yolks; beat further
20 seconds. Transfer
mixture to a large
mixing bowl.
6 Fold in milk and
sifted ingredients
quickly and lightly.
7 Spread mixture
evenly in prepared tin;
smooth surface. Bake
for 8 minutes or until
springy to the touch.

8 Sprinkle a large
sheet of greaseproof
paper with the extra
sugar. Turn the cake
onto the paper; let
stand 1 minute.
Discard the cake tin
lining paper. Trim ends
of roll with serrated
knife. Carefully roll
cake up with paper;
stand cake 5 minutes
or until cool.
9 Whip cream with
extra coffee powder.
Fold through half the
crumbled chocolate and
all the flaked almonds.
Unroll cake, spread with
most of the cream
mixture; re-roll using
greaseproof paper as a
guide, if necessary, to
help you. Carefully place
cake on serving plate.
Decorate with the
remaining cream and
crumbled chocolate.

Note: 6 tablespoons
flour is equal to 1/2 cup.

Mocha Swiss Roll.

1. *For Mocha Swiss Roll: Beat egg whites*
until soft peaks form, add sugar gradually.

2. *Fold in milk and sifted ingredients,*
quickly and lightly.

3. Roll up unfilled cake carefully, using the paper to ensure it is neat and compact.

4. Spread cake with cream mixture and re-roll, using paper as a guide if necessary.

Chocolate Ginger Cake

Preparation time:
  25 minutes
Cooking time:
  35 minutes
Makes 1 x 23 cm round
  cake

60 g butter
½ cup caster sugar
2 eggs, lightly beaten
1 tablespoon golden
  syrup
1 cup self-raising flour,
  sifted
2 teaspoons ground
  ginger
½ teaspoon
  bicarbonate of soda,
  sifted
¼ cup cocoa, sifted
¾ cup milk

Icing
50 g butter
⅓ cup icing sugar
1 tablespoon cocoa
1 tablespoon glacé
  ginger, finely chopped

1 Preheat oven to
180°C. Brush deep 23 cm
round cake tin with
melted butter or oil,
line base and side with
paper; grease paper.
2 Beat butter and sugar
with electric beaters in
small mixer bowl until
light and creamy. Add
eggs gradually, beating
thoroughly after each
addition. Add golden
syrup; beat until
thoroughly combined.
3 Transfer mixture to
large mixing bowl.
Using a metal spoon,
fold in sifted dry
ingredients alternately
with milk. Stir until just
combined and mixture
is almost smooth.
4 Spoon mixture into
prepared tin; smooth
surface. Bake 35 minutes
or until skewer comes
out clean when inserted
in centre of cake.
5 Stand cake in tin 10
minutes before turning
onto wire rack to cool.
6 To make Icing: Beat

butter and sugar with
electric beaters in small
mixer bowl until light
and creamy. Add cocoa,
beat until combined;
stir in ginger. Spread
icing evenly over cake
using a palette knife.

Chocolate and Walnut Buttercake

Preparation time:
  20 minutes
Cooking time:
  30 minutes
Makes 1 x 19 cm
  square cake

125 g butter
½ cup caster sugar
2 eggs, lightly beaten
1 teaspoon imitation
  vanilla essence
½ cup walnuts,
  chopped
2 cups self-raising flour,
  sifted
2 tablespoons cocoa,
  sifted
½ cup milk

Icing
50 g butter
⅓ cup icing sugar, sifted
1 tablespoon cocoa,
  sifted
walnut halves, for
  decoration

1 Preheat oven to
180°C. Brush a deep
19 cm square tin with
melted butter or oil,
line base and sides with
paper; grease paper.

HINT
For cake making, butter is preferable to
margarine. Butter gives the best flavour and
improves the keeping qualities of the cake.
However, margarine is an acceptable substitute,
and will still produce a good result.
When you're using small amounts of butter or
liquid that require melting or heating, don't
bother with the stove – make use of your
microwave for a speedy result.
When folding ingredients into a cake batter, do
so with a very light hand. This is important to
ensure maximum rising of the finished cake.

Chocolate and Walnut Buttercake (left), Chocolate Ginger Cake.

2 Beat butter and sugar with electric beaters in small mixer bowl until light and creamy. Add eggs gradually, beating thoroughly after each addition. Add essence, beat until combined.
3 Transfer mixture to large mixing bowl; add walnuts. Using a metal spoon, fold in sifted dry ingredients alternately with milk. Stir until just combined and mixture is almost smooth.
4 Spoon mixture into prepared tin; smooth surface. Bake 30 minutes or until skewer comes out clean when inserted in centre of cake.
5 Stand cake in tin 10 minutes before turning onto wire rack to cool.
6 To make Icing: Beat butter with electric beaters in small mixer bowl until light and creamy. Add sifted icing sugar and cocoa; beat until combined. Spread icing evenly over cake using a palette knife. Decorate with walnut halves.

15

Chocolate and Cherry Layer Cake

Preparation time:
 30 minutes
Cooking time:
 30 minutes
Makes 1 x 23 cm layer cake

3 cups self-raising flour
1¼ cups caster sugar
2 tablespoons cocoa
200 g dark chocolate, chopped
1½ cups milk
3 eggs, lightly beaten
185 g butter, softened
1 x 425 g can pitted cherries, drained and chopped

Chocolate Mock Cream
¾ cup caster sugar
⅓ cup water
80 g dark chocolate, chopped
125 g butter
1 tablespoon cherry brandy, optional

1 Preheat oven to 180°C. Brush two deep 23 cm round cake tins with melted butter or oil, line base and sides with paper; grease paper.
2 Sift first three ingredients into large mixer bowl.
3 Place chocolate in glass bowl. Stir over barely simmering water until melted; remove from heat.

4 Pour combined milk and eggs onto dry ingredients; beat on low speed for 2 minutes until just moistened. Add butter and melted chocolate.
5 Beat mixture on high speed for 5 minutes or until it is free of lumps and increased in volume. Stir in cherries.
6 Pour mixture evenly into prepared tins; smooth surface. Bake 30 minutes or until skewer comes out clean when inserted in centre of cakes.
7 Stand cakes in tins 10 minutes before turning onto wire rack to cool.
8 To make Chocolate Mock Cream: Combine sugar and water in small pan. Stir over low heat until sugar has dissolved. Simmer 5 minutes; remove from heat; cool. Melt chocolate as for Step 3. Beat butter with electric beaters in small mixer bowl until light and creamy. Pour cooled syrup in a thin stream over creamed butter, beating constantly. Add chocolate and cherry brandy; beat until glossy and smooth.
9 Cut each cake in half horizontally. Place first cake layer on a board. Spread cake evenly with chocolate mock cream. Continue layering with

remaining cake and cream, ending with cream on top. Transfer to serving plate.

Note: This cake may also be assembled on the serving plate.

Triple Choc Cake

Preparation time:
 20 minutes
Cooking time:
 35 minutes
Makes 1 x 19 cm square cake

125 g butter, softened
⅔ cup caster sugar
⅓ cup icing sugar
1¼ cups self-raising flour
½ cup cocoa
1 teaspoon bicarbonate of soda
2 eggs, lightly beaten
1 cup milk
1 teaspoon imitation vanilla essence
⅓ cup Choc Bits

Icing
⅔ cup Choc Bits
30 g butter
1 cup icing sugar
2 tablespoons hot water

1 Preheat oven to 180°C. Brush a deep 19 cm square tin with melted butter or oil, line base and sides with paper; grease paper.
2 Beat butter and sugars with electric beaters in small mixer

Chocolate and Cherry Layer Cake (left), Triple Choc Cake.

bowl until light and creamy.

3 Transfer mixture to large mixing bowl. Add sifted flour, cocoa and bicarbonate of soda alternately with combined eggs and milk. Beat until smooth.

4 Using metal spoon, fold in essence and Choc Bits.

5 Spoon mixture into prepared tin; smooth surface. Bake 40 minutes or until skewer comes out clean when inserted in centre of cake.

6 Stand the cake in the tin 5 minutes before turning onto wire rack to cool.

7 To make Icing: Combine Choc Bits and butter in a small pan. Stir constantly over low heat. Add icing sugar, beat until icing is thick. Add enough hot water to make the icing spreadable and smooth. Spread icing evenly over cake using a palette knife to make surface smooth. Decorate with silver balls (optional).

HINT

Wrap chocolate and store it in a cool, dry place. Don't be tempted to store it in the refrigerator – it will tend to develop an unattractive, whiteish 'bloom', making it unusable for decorations.

Chocolate Apricot Sponge

Preparation time:
  30 minutes
Cooking time:
  20 minutes
Makes 1 double sponge

4 eggs
⅔ cup caster sugar
⅔ cup plain flour
2 tablespoons cocoa
100 g butter, melted

Filling
200 g dried apricots
400 ml coconut cream

Topping
½ cup cream, whipped
1-2 tablespoons flaked
  almonds, toasted

1 Preheat oven to
180°C. Brush two
shallow 20 cm round
cake tins with melted
butter or oil, line base
and sides with paper;
grease paper.
2 Beat eggs with
electric beaters in small
mixer bowl until thick
and pale.
3 Add sugar gradually,
beating constantly until
mixture is pale yellow
and all sugar is
dissolved. Transfer to
large mixing bowl.
4 Sift dry ingredients
three times onto
greaseproof paper.

5 Using a metal spoon,
fold in butter and dry
ingredients quickly and
lightly.
6 Spread mixture
evenly into prepared
tins. Bake for 20
minutes or until sponge
shrinks from side of tins.
7 Stand sponge in tins
for 5 minutes before
turning onto wire rack
to cool.
8 To make Filling:
Combine apricots and
coconut cream in a
medium pan. Simmer
over low heat until
apricots have absorbed
the coconut cream and
are plump; stir
occasionally. Remove
from heat. Place apricot
mixture in processor
bowl. Using the pulse
action, process until
smooth. Allow mixture
to cool.
9 Sandwich sponges
together with filling.
Spread cream evenly
over top of sponge and
sprinkle with toasted,
flaked almonds.

HINT
Store nuts in airtight
containers. Purchase
them in small
amounts sufficient
for your needs.
Because of their oil
content, nuts have a
tendency to go rancid
in warm weather.

Chocolate Apricot Sponge, Double Chocolate Cake.

Double Chocolate Cake

Preparation time:
25 minutes
Cooking time:
20 minutes
Makes 1 double layer cake

60 g white chocolate, chopped
155 g butter
1/2 cup caster sugar
2 eggs, lightly beaten
2/3 cup self-raising flour, sifted
2 tablespoons cocoa, sifted

Filling
100 g dark chocolate, chopped
60 g butter
3/4 cup icing sugar

Icing
1/2 cup icing sugar
1 tablespoon cocoa
1 tablespoon milk

1 Preheat oven to 180°C. Brush two shallow 20 cm round cake tins with melted butter or oil, line base and sides with paper; grease paper.
2 Place chocolate in glass bowl. Stir over barely simmering water until melted; remove from heat.
3 Beat butter and sugar in small mixer bowl until light and creamy.

Add eggs gradually, beating thoroughly after each addition. Add chocolate; beat until combined.
4 Transfer mixture to large mixing bowl. Using a metal spoon, fold in sifted ingredients. Stir until just combined and mixture is almost smooth.
5 Spoon mixture evenly into prepared tins; smooth surface. Bake 20 minutes or until skewer comes out clean when inserted in centre of cakes.
6 Stand cakes in tins 5 minutes before turning onto wire rack to cool.
7 To make Filling: Melt chocolate as for Step 2. Beat butter with electric beaters in small mixer bowl until light and creamy. Add icing sugar gradually, beating thoroughly after each addition. Add chocolate, beat until combined.
8 To make Icing: Sift dry ingredients into small mixing bowl, blend in milk; stir until smooth.
9 Sandwich cakes together with filling. Spread icing evenly over top of cake, using a palette knife to make it smooth. Decorate with chocolate curls.

Chocolate and Sultana Cake

Preparation time:
20 minutes
Cooking time:
40 minutes
Makes 1 x 23 cm square cake

200 g butter
1 cup caster sugar
2 eggs, lightly beaten
2 teaspoons imitation vanilla essence
2 tablespoons brandy or milk
1/2 cup sultanas
2 cups self-raising flour, sifted
1/3 cup cocoa, sifted
1 cup milk

Icing
1/4 cup cream
100 g dark chocolate, chopped

1 Preheat oven to 180°C. Brush a deep 23 cm square cake tin with melted butter or oil, line base and sides with paper; grease paper.
2 Beat butter and sugar with electric beaters in small mixer bowl until light and creamy. Add eggs gradually, beating well after each addition. Add essence and brandy; beat until combined.

Clockwise from top: Chocolate and Sultana Cake, Chocolate Pecan Tea Cake (recipe page 22), Chocolate Butterflies (recipe page 22).

1. For Chocolate Butterflies: Use metal spoon to fold in chocolate and flour.

2. Spoon heaped tablespoons of mixture into patty cases.

3 Transfer mixture to large mixing bowl; add sultanas. Using a metal spoon, fold in sifted ingredients alternately with the milk. Stir until just combined and the mixture is almost smooth.

4 Spoon mixture into prepared tin; smooth surface. Bake 1 hour or until skewer comes out clean when inserted in centre of cake.

5 Stand cake in tin 10 minutes before turning onto wire rack to cool.

6 To make Icing: Combine cream and chocolate in a small pan. Stir over low heat until the mixture is smooth; remove from heat. Spread icing evenly over cake using a palette knife.

HINT
Place chocolate in fridge for 30 minutes before grating.

Chocolate Butterflies

Preparation time:
  20 minutes
Cooking time:
  10 minutes
Makes 32 patty cakes

125 g butter
½ cup caster sugar
2 eggs
1 teaspoon imitation
  vanilla essence
100 g dark chocolate,
  grated
2 cups self-raising flour,
  sifted
½ cup milk
2 tablespoons chocolate
  topping
1 cup cream
1 tablespoon icing sugar
1 tablespoon cocoa or
  drinking chocolate

1 Preheat oven to 180°C. Line deep patty tins with patty cases.

2 Beat butter and sugar with electric beaters in small mixer bowl until light and creamy. Add eggs gradually, beating thoroughly after each addition. Add essence; beat until combined.

3 Transfer mixture to large mixing bowl; add grated chocolate. Using a metal spoon, fold in sifted flour alternately with milk. Stir until just combined and the mixture is almost smooth.

4 Spoon heaped tablespoons of mixture into patty tins. Bake for 10 minutes or until skewer comes out clean when inserted in centre of cakes.

5 Stand patty cakes in tins for 5 minutes before turning onto wire rack to cool. Line tins again with patty cases; repeat cooking procedure with remaining mixture.

6 When patty cakes are cold, cut out a small circle from the top of

3. Cut a small circle from the top of each cake, cutting down to a depth of 2 cm.

4. Cut small circle in half to make 'wings'. Place on cream-filled cakes.

each one, cutting down to a depth of about 2 cm to allow for filling. Cut small cake slice in half to make 'wings'.

7 Stir chocolate topping into whipped cream. Spoon a heaped teaspoonful of cream into patty cakes. Top with 'wings'. Dust with combined icing sugar and drinking chocolate.

Chocolate Pecan Tea Cake

Preparation time:
  25 minutes
Cooking time:
  35 minutes
Makes 1 x 23 cm round cake

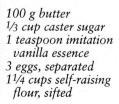

100 g butter
1/3 cup caster sugar
1 teaspoon imitation
  vanilla essence
3 eggs, separated
1 1/4 cups self-raising
  flour, sifted

2/3 cup milk
1/4 cup Choc Bits
1/4 cup pecans, chopped
icing sugar

1 Preheat oven to 180°C. Brush a 23 cm flan tin with melted butter or oil. Coat the base and side evenly with flour; shake off any excess.

2 Beat butter, sugar and essence in small mixer bowl at medium speed until light and creamy. Add lightly beaten egg yolks, beat until just combined.

3 Add flour and milk gradually, beat at low speed 1 minute or until mixture is smooth.

Transfer mixture to large mixing bowl.

4 Place egg whites in a small mixer bowl. Beat until soft peaks form. Fold egg whites into flour mixture. Stir until just combined.

5 Spread half the mixture in base of prepared tin. Sprinkle on Choc Bits and pecans. Spread the remaining mixture over the top. Bake 35 minutes or until skewer comes out clean when inserted in the centre of the cake.

6 Stand cake in tin 10 minutes before turning onto wire rack to cool. Dust cake with icing sugar, to serve.

HINT
Chocolate is available in dark, milk and white varieties. The white variety is a mixture only of cocoa butter, milk solids and sugar. It contains no cocoa solids, which accounts for its pale, creamy white appearance. White chocolate looks most attractive when it is contrasted with a milk or dark variety in cooking.

Quick mixes

F ood processors and electric beaters have helped reduce tedious preparation time spent in the kitchen. As well, they have proved themselves invaluable in producing volume, lightness and a softness of texture that elbow grease alone cannot hope to achieve. For cake making, these assets are much valued by the busy cook.

The time-saving recipes in this section use some interesting combinations of ingredients that result in a deliciously different range of flavours and textures. Try the smooth-textured Chocolate Yoghurt Cake or the Tipsy Mocha Cake with its dash of coffee liqueur.

Chocolate Mud Cake

Preparation time:
  15 minutes
Cooking time:
  1½ hours
*Makes one 23 cm
  round or square cake*

1⅓ *cups self-raising
  flour*
⅓ *cup plain flour*
⅓ *cup cocoa*
1 *cup caster sugar*
200 *g butter*
250 *g dark chocolate,
  chopped*

⅓ *cup hot water*
3 *eggs*

Icing
200 *g dark chocolate,
  chopped*
100 *g unsalted butter*
2 *tablespoons cream*
whipped cream, extra

1 Preheat oven to 160°C. Brush a deep 23 cm round or square cake tin with melted butter or oil. Line base and side/s with paper; grease paper.
2 Sift the flours and cocoa into a large mixing bowl. Make a

*Chocolate Mud Cake (top), Choc Lemon
Buttercake (recipe page 26).*

well in the centre.

3 Combine sugar, butter, chocolate and water in a medium pan. Stir over low heat until butter and chocolate have melted and sugar has dissolved; remove from heat.

4 Add butter mixture and eggs to dry ingredients. Stir with wooden spoon until ingredients are just combined; do not overbeat.

5 Pour mixture into prepared tin. Bake 1½ hours or until skewer comes out clean when inserted in the centre of the cake.

6 Stand cake in tin 20 minutes before turning onto wire rack to cool.

7 To make Icing: Combine chocolate, butter and cream in small pan. Stir over low heat until chocolate and butter have melted; remove from heat. Cool.

8 Spread the icing over cake. Serve with whipped cream.

HINT

Chocolate (properly stored in a cool, dry place), will keep in good condition for about a year. That assumes, of course, that your family can keep their hands off it for that long.

Choc Lemon Buttercake

Preparation time:
 25 minutes
Cooking time:
 30 minutes
Makes one 30 x 20 cm slab cake

150 g white chocolate, chopped
250 g butter
¾ cup caster sugar
3 eggs
2 teaspoons grated lemon rind
2 tablespoons lemon juice
2½ cups self-raising flour, sifted
¼ cup milk

Icing
1 tablespoon lemon juice
½ cup icing sugar, sifted
1 teaspoon butter, softened
60 g white chocolate, chopped

1 Preheat oven to 180°C. Brush a shallow 30 x 20 cm cake tin with melted butter or oil, line base and sides with paper; grease paper.

2 Place chocolate in glass bowl. Stir over barely simmering water until melted; remove from heat.

3 Beat butter and sugar with electric beaters in medium mixer bowl until light and creamy. Add eggs gradually, beating thoroughly after each addition. Add rind, juice and melted chocolate; beat until combined.

4 Add sifted flour alternately with milk; beat until smooth.

5 Pour mixture into prepared tin; smooth surface. Bake 30 minutes or until skewer comes out clean when inserted in centre of cake.

6 Stand cake in tin 10 minutes before turning onto wire rack to cool.

7 To make Icing: Combine lemon juice with icing sugar in a small mixing bowl. Add butter, stir until combined. Spread icing evenly over cake using a palette knife.

8 Melt chocolate as for Step 2 and drizzle or pipe in a lattice pattern over iced cake.

HINT

When melting chocolate, don't let a droplet of water fall on it. A small amount of liquid can turn it suddenly into a stiff mass, whereas if you add a larger amount, it should blend in smoothly. Don't overheat the chocolate; it will turn dull and grainy.

Tipsy Mocha Cake

Preparation time:
  20 minutes
Cooking time:
  20 minutes
*Makes 1 x 20 cm ring
  cake*

Cake
250 g butter, softened
1 cup caster sugar
4 eggs
2 cups wholemeal or
  white self-raising
  flour, sifted
1/2 cup cocoa, sifted

Syrup
1 tablespoon caster
  sugar
2 teaspoons instant
  coffee powder
3 tablespoons boiling
  water
2 tablespoons
  coffee-flavoured
  liqueur, or brandy

Decoration
1 cup cream
thin chocolate-coated
  wafer biscuits

Tipsy Mocha Cake.

1 Preheat oven to 180°C. Brush a deep, 20 cm ring tin with melted butter or oil. Coat base and side evenly with flour; shake off any excess.
2 Beat butter and sugar with electric beaters in small mixer bowl until light and creamy. Add eggs gradually, beating well after each addition.
3 Transfer mixture to large mixing bowl. Using a metal spoon, fold in sifted ingredients. Stir until just combined and the mixture is almost smooth.
4 Spoon mixture into prepared tin; smooth surface. Bake for 20 minutes or until skewer comes out clean when inserted in the centre of the cake.
5 Stand cake in tin 5 minutes before turning onto wire rack and carefully removing ring tin. Spoon the syrup over the cake while still warm.
6 To make Syrup: Dissolve sugar and coffee in boiling water; stir in liqueur.
7 To decorate, beat cream until it is just stiff. Spoon about 4 tablespoons into piping bag with large star tube, reserve. Spread remainder evenly over the cake. Pipe reserved cream on top; garnish with wafers. Chill until ready to serve.

HINT
Melt chocolate in the microwave in a single layer on Medium for 30 seconds. Remove, stir vigorously. If still not melted, return to the microwave on High for 10 seconds.

27

Black Magic Cake

Preparation time:
  25 minutes
Cooking time:
  55 minutes
Makes 1 x 20 cm ring
  cake

1 cup caster sugar
2 eggs
1 teaspoon imitation
  vanilla essence
1³/4 cups self-raising
  flour
²/3 cup cocoa
1 teaspoon bicarbonate
  of soda
1 tablespoon instant
  coffee powder
³/4 cup water
³/4 cup buttermilk
¹/4 cup vegetable oil

Icing
200 g dark chocolate,
  chopped
²/3 cup cream
30 g butter

1 Preheat oven to
180°C. Brush deep
20 cm (4 cup capacity)
ring tin with melted
butter or oil. Coat base
and side evenly with
flour; shake off excess.
2 Beat sugar and eggs
with electric beaters in a
large mixer bowl until
thick and creamy. Add
essence, beat until it is
combined.
3 Add the sifted dry
ingredients alternately
with liquids. Beat until

mixture is smooth and
free of lumps.
4 Pour mixture into
prepared tin. Bake
55 minutes or until
skewer comes out clean
when inserted in centre
of cake.
5 Stand cake in tin 20
minutes before turning
onto wire rack to cool.
6 To make Icing:
Combine chocolate,
cream and butter in a
small pan. Stir over low
heat until smooth.
Remove from heat;
cool slightly.
7 Pour icing over cake.
Add chocolate curls.

> **HINT**
> The Swiss are the
> champion chocolate
> eaters – they munch
> 10 kilos per capita
> per annum.

Beat it, Bake it Chocolate Cake

Preparation time:
  15 minutes
Cooking time:
  35 minutes
Makes 1 x 23 cm ring cake

1¹/3 cups plain flour
1 cup caster sugar
²/3 cup cocoa
1 teaspoon bicarbonate
  of soda

2 eggs, lightly beaten
1 cup buttermilk
125 g butter, softened
1¹/2 teaspoons imitation
  vanilla essence
300 ml cream, whipped
1 tablespoon chocolate
  topping

1 Preheat oven to
180°C. Brush the tin/s
with melted butter or
oil, line the base and
sides with paper; grease
the paper.
2 Sift flour with
remaining dry
ingredients into large
mixer bowl. Make a
well in the centre.
3 Pour combined eggs,
buttermilk, butter and
vanilla onto dry
ingredients, beat on low
speed for 30 seconds.
4 Beat mixture on high
speed for 3 minutes or
until mixture is free of
lumps and increased in
volume.
5 Pour mixture into
prepared tin. Bake for
35 minutes or until
skewer comes out clean
when inserted in centre
of cake.
6 Stand cake in tin for
5 minutes before
turning onto wire rack
to cool. Combine the
whipped cream and
chocolate topping.
Spread mixture over
cake. Top with grated
chocolate curls.

Black Magic Cake (top), Beat it, Bake it
Chocolate Cake.

Jaffa Cake

Preparation time:
  20 minutes
Cooking time:
  35 minutes
Makes 1 x 23 cm round
  cake

185 g butter
½ cup caster sugar
2 eggs
1 teaspoon grated
  orange rind
½ cup sour cream
1¾ cup self-raising
  flour, sifted
⅓ cup cocoa, sifted
⅓ cup orange juice

Icing
100 g chocolate,
  chopped
50 g butter
¼ cup icing sugar

1 Preheat oven to
180°C. Brush a deep
23 cm round cake tin
with melted butter or
oil, line base and side
with paper; grease paper.
2 Beat butter and sugar
with electric beaters in
medium mixer bowl
until light and creamy.
Add eggs gradually,
beating thoroughly
after each addition.
Add rind and sour
cream; beat to combine.
3 Add sifted
ingredients alternately
with orange juice; beat

mixture until smooth.
4 Pour mixture into
prepared tin; smooth
the surface. Bake 35
minutes or until skewer
comes out clean when
inserted in centre of cake.
5 Stand cake in tin 10
minutes before turning
onto wire rack to cool.
6 To make Icing: Place
chocolate in glass bowl.
Stir over barely
simmering water until
melted; remove from
heat. Beat butter and
sugar with electric
beaters in small mixer
bowl until light and
creamy. Add chocolate;
beat until combined.
Spread evenly over cake.

Chocolate Brownie Cake

Preparation time:
  15 minutes
Cooking time:
  25 minutes
Makes 1 x 20 cm round
  cake

100 g dark chocolate,
  chopped
⅔ cup plain flour
2 tablespoons cocoa
½ cup caster sugar
2 eggs
1 tablespoon cream
90 g butter, melted
½ cup flaked almonds
whipped cream, extra,
  to serve

Jaffa Cake (top) and Chocolate Brownie Cake.

1 Preheat oven to 170°C. Brush deep 20 cm round springform tin with melted butter or oil, line base and side with paper; grease paper.
2 Place chocolate in glass bowl. Stir over barely simmering water until melted; remove from heat.
3 Place flour, cocoa and sugar in food-processor bowl. Add remaining ingredients except almonds. Using the pulse action, process 15 seconds or until mixture is smooth.
4 Pour mixture into prepared tin; smooth surface. Sprinkle over almonds. Bake for 25 minutes or until skewer comes out clean when inserted in centre of cake.
5 Stand cake in tin for 10 minutes before turning onto wire rack to cool. Cut into wedges and serve with freshly whipped cream.

> ### HINT
> Chocolate contains some essential nutrients: proteins, carbohydrates and fats. Milk chocolate also contains vitamins A, B_1, B_2, D and E, as well as phosphorus, calcium, magnesium and traces of iron and copper.

Chocolate Banana Cake

Preparation time:
  15 minutes
Cooking time:
  30 minutes
Makes two bar cakes
26 x 8 x 4.5 cm

2 cups self-raising flour
1/4 cup cocoa
1 cup caster sugar
1/4 teaspoon bicarbonate of soda
2 eggs
3/4 cup boiling water
1 teaspoon imitation vanilla essence
2 bananas, peeled and roughly broken

Icing
100 g cream cheese
1/2 cup icing sugar
1 tablespoon hot milk
1 tablespoon cocoa

1 Preheat oven to 180°C. Brush two 26 x 8 x 4.5 cm long bar tins with melted butter or oil, line base with paper; grease paper.
2 Place dry ingredients into food-processor bowl. Add eggs, water, essence and banana. Using the pulse action, process 15 seconds or until mixture is smooth.
3 Spoon mixture into prepared tins; smooth surfaces. Bake for 30 minutes or until skewer comes out clean

when inserted in centre.
4 Stand cakes in tins 10 minutes before turning onto wire rack to cool.
5 To make Icing: Beat cream cheese and icing sugar with electric beaters in small mixer bowl until smooth and creamy. Add milk and cocoa; beat until well combined. Spread evenly over cakes using a palette knife.

Chocolate Yoghurt Cake

Preparation time:
  15 minutes
Cooking time:
  50 minutes
Makes 1 x 23 cm round or square cake

1 1/2 cups self-raising flour
1/2 cup cocoa
1 cup caster sugar
200 g plain yoghurt
2 eggs
200 g butter, melted

Icing
50 g dark chocolate, chopped
50 g butter
1/2 cup icing sugar
2 tablespoons yoghurt

1 Preheat oven to 180°C. Brush a deep 23 cm tin with melted butter or oil, line base and sides with paper; grease paper.

Chocolate Yoghurt Cake (left), Chocolate Banana Cake.

2 Place dry ingredients into food-processor bowl. Add yoghurt, eggs and butter. Using the pulse action, process 15 seconds or until the mixture is smooth.
3 Pour mixture into prepared tin; smooth surface. Bake for 50 minutes or until skewer comes out clean when inserted in centre of cake.
4 Stand cake in tin 10 minutes before turning onto wire rack to cool.
5 To make Icing: Place chocolate in glass bowl. Stir over barely simmering water until melted; remove from heat. Beat butter and icing sugar with electric beaters in small bowl until smooth and creamy. Add chocolate and yoghurt; beat well until combined. Spread the mixture evenly over the cake using a palette knife.

33

1. For Moist Jam Cake: Sift flours, bicarbonate of soda and cocoa into bowl.

2. Combine the butter, sugar, water and jam in a small pan.

Moist Jam Cake

Preparation time:
  15 minutes
Cooking time:
  35 minutes
*Makes 1 x 23 cm round
  cake*

1 *cup self-raising flour*
¼ *cup plain flour*
¼ *teaspoon
  bicarbonate of soda*
¼ *cup cocoa*
100 *g butter*
⅔ *cup sugar*
⅓ *cup jam (any flavour)*
⅓ *cup hot water*
2 *eggs, lightly beaten*
1 *tablespoon jam, extra*
whipped cream, to serve

1 Preheat oven to
170°C. Brush a deep
23 cm round tin with
melted butter or oil,
line base and side with
paper; grease paper.
2 Sift the flours,
bicarbonate of soda and
cocoa into large mixing
bowl. Make a well in
the centre.
3 Combine butter,
sugar, jam and water in
a small pan. Stir over
low heat until butter
has melted and sugar
has dissolved; remove
from heat.
4 Add butter mixture
and eggs to dry
ingredients. Stir with a
wooden spoon until just
combined; do not
overbeat.
5 Pour mixture into
prepared tin; smooth
surface. Bake for
35 minutes or until
skewer comes out clean
when inserted in centre
of cake.
6 Stand cake in tin 15
minutes before turning
onto wire rack to cool.
7 Heat extra jam in a
small pan. Brush hot
jam on cake. Serve cake
with whipped cream.

Moist Jam Cake.

*3. Add the butter mixture and the eggs to
the dry ingredients.*

*4. Heat extra jam and brush it over the
surface of the cake.*

Celebration specials

Pull out all the stops when you entertain. Allow the time to create that memorable treat that befits the occasion. When a celebration is in order, it's perfectly acceptable to err on the side of indulgence.

Many of the cakes featured here can easily double as dinner party desserts – they are beautifully decorated and will make suitably stunning centrepieces. Some may require more dexterity in the preparation than others, but the results will repay the effort. Chocoholics will find it impossible to resist Chocolate and Creamy Berry Roulade or Ganache Torte.

Chocolate Almond Torte

Preparation time:
  20 minutes
Cooking time:
  1 hour 20 minutes
Makes 1 x 20 cm torte

125 g milk chocolate, chopped
¼ cup boiling water
4 eggs, separated
½ teaspoon almond essence
180 g butter
1½ cups brown sugar
1⅓ cups self-raising flour, sifted
3 tablespoons milk

2 tablespoons cocoa, sifted
2 tablespoons ground almonds

Topping
180 g milk chocolate, chopped
½ cup cream
12 chocolate-coated almonds
cocoa
60 g milk chocolate, grated

Filling
½ cup cream, whipped

1 Preheat oven to 180°C. Grease a round 20 cm springform tin with melted butter or oil,

Chocolate Mousse Torte (front, recipe page 38), Chocolate Almond Torte.

1. *For Chocolate Mousse Torte: Shake excess flour from recess flan tin.*

2. *Beat eggs and sugar until mixture is pale yellow and glossy and sugar is dissolved.*

line base and side with paper; grease paper.

2 Place chocolate and water in glass bowl. Stir over barely simmering water until melted; remove from heat. Add egg yolks and essence.

3 Beat butter and sugar with electric beaters in small mixer bowl until light and fluffy. Add chocolate mixture; beat until combined. Transfer mixture to large mixing bowl. Using a metal spoon, fold in sifted ingredients and almonds alternately with milk.

4 Place egg whites in a small, clean and dry mixer bowl. Beat until soft peaks form. Fold into mixture quickly and lightly.

5 Spoon mixture into prepared tin; smooth surface. Bake for 40 minutes; reduce oven to 160°C and bake a further 40 minutes or until skewer comes out clean when inserted in

centre of cake. Stand cake in tin 5 minutes before turning onto wire rack to cool. Cut cake horizontally into three even slices.

6 To make Topping: Place chocolate in glass bowl. Stir over barely simmering water until melted; remove from heat. Mix in cream.

7 To make Filling: Combine 1 tablespoon of topping with whipped cream.

8 Place first cake layer on a board. Spread cake evenly with half the filling. Layer with remaining cake and filling, ending with cake on top. Transfer to serving plate. Using a palette knife, cover top and sides evenly with the topping. Mark the top into wedges. Dust chocolate-coated almonds with cocoa. Place 1 almond on each wedge. Press grated chocolate onto sides.

Chocolate Mousse Torte

Preparation time:
  30 minutes
Cooking time:
  20 minutes
Makes 1 x 23 cm round cake

1/3 cup plain flour
2 tablespoons cocoa
2 eggs
1/3 cup caster sugar
50 g dark chocolate, chopped
50 g butter, melted

Mousse
150 g dark chocolate
1/4 cup water
2 tablespoons caster sugar
2 egg yolks
1 teaspoon melted butter
3/4 cup cream, whipped
2 teaspoons crème de cacao
1/2 teaspoon gelatine
1 tablespoon hot water

3. *Place chocolate in glass bowl. Stir over barely simmering water until melted.*

4. *To make Mousse: Whisk egg yolks and butter into chocolate mixture.*

Decoration
60 g white chocolate, chopped
60 g dark chocolate, chopped

1 Preheat oven to 180°C. Brush a 23 cm recess flan tin with melted butter or oil. Coat base and sides evenly with flour; shake off any excess.
2 Sift flour and cocoa three times onto greaseproof paper. Beat eggs with electric beaters in small mixer bowl until thick and pale. Add sugar gradually, beating constantly until mixture is pale yellow and glossy and all the sugar is dissolved. Transfer the mixture to large mixing bowl.
3 Place chocolate in glass bowl. Stir over barely simmering water until melted; remove from heat. Using a metal spoon, fold the melted chocolate,

the butter and the dry ingredients into the egg mixture quickly and lightly.
4 Spread mixture evenly in prepared tin. Bake for 20 minutes or until sponge shrinks away from side of tin. Stand sponge in tin for 5 minutes before turning onto wire rack to cool.
5 To make Mousse: Combine chocolate, water and sugar in a small pan. Stir over low heat until the chocolate has melted and the sugar has dissolved; remove pan from heat. Transfer mixture to large mixing bowl. Whisk in egg yolks and butter. Beat mixture until thick and doubled in quantity. Fold in the cream and crème de cacao. Dissolve the gelatine in hot water. Whisk into the chocolate mixture.
6 Spread chocolate

mousse evenly onto the sponge base. Refrigerate until set. Melt the white and dark chocolate separately as for Step 3 and drizzle them attractively over the top of the cake.

Luscious Black Forest Cherry Cake
Preparation time:
  40 minutes
Cooking time:
  35 minutes
Makes 1 x 23 cm round cake

1 x 370 g packet chocolate cake mix or use your own recipe
1 x 425 g tin pitted sour cherries
1 tablespoon gelatine
2 tablespoons hot water
2 tablespoons kirsch
2 cups cream, whipped
1/2 cup flaked almonds
chocolate curls, for decoration (see page 4)

39

Luscious Black Forest Cherry Cake (recipe page 39).

1 Brush a deep 23 cm round cake tin with melted butter or oil, line base and side with paper; grease paper. Prepare and bake cake following the packet instructions.

2 Drain cherries. Reserve ½ cup liquid. Cut cherries in half. Sprinkle gelatine over hot water. Whisk vigorously using a fork to dissolve. Add to combined reserved liquid and kirsch. Cool slightly. *You must not allow it to set.*

3 Cut cake horizontally into three even slices. Place first cake layer on serving plate. Spread cake evenly with half the gelatine mixture.

4 Divide cream into three portions. Using a metal spoon, fold cherries through one third of the cream. Spread cake evenly with cherried cream, using a palette knife.

5 Top with second cake layer. Spread evenly with remaining gelatine mixture followed by a portion of plain cream. Top with third cake layer. Cover the top and sides with the remaining cream. Press almonds on side of cake. Decorate with chocolate curls (see page 4 for instructions on how to make these and other decorations).

Chocolate and Creamy Berry Roulade

Preparation time:
30 minutes
Cooking time:
15 minutes
Makes 1 roulade

60 g dark chocolate, chopped
4 eggs
3/4 cup caster sugar
1 teaspoon imitation vanilla essence
1/2 cup plain flour, sifted
1/2 teaspoon baking powder, sifted
2 tablespoons cold water

Chocolate and Creamy Berry Roulade.

½ teaspoon
  bicarbonate of soda
icing sugar, sifted

Filling
1 cup cream, whipped
1 x 250 g punnet fresh
raspberries, sliced
in half

1 Preheat oven to
200°C. Brush a shallow
30 x 25 x 2 cm Swiss roll
tin with melted butter or
oil. Line base and two
sides with paper; grease
paper.
2 Place chocolate in
glass bowl. Stir over
barely simmering water
until melted; remove
from heat.
3 Beat eggs with electric
beaters in small mixer

bowl until thick and
pale. Add sugar
gradually, beating
constantly until mixture
is pale yellow and glossy
and all the sugar is
dissolved. Stir in essence.
Transfer mixture to large
mixing bowl. Using a
metal spoon, fold in
the sifted flour and
baking powder quickly
and lightly.
4 Stir the water and
bicarbonate of soda into
cooled chocolate until
smooth. Fold into flour
mixture. Spread mixture
evenly into prepared tin;
smooth surface. Bake
15 minutes or until
springy to the touch.
Turn onto a dry tea-towel
covered with greaseproof

paper; stand 1 minute.
Using the tea-towel as a
guide, carefully roll
cake up with paper;
stand 5 minutes or until
cool. Unroll cake,
discard paper.
5 Spread cake with
cream and cover with the
fruit; re-roll. Trim ends
of roll with serrated
knife; dust with icing
sugar to serve.

HINT
Cake must be at
room temperature
before you store it.
It's important that
the container is close
fitting in order to
minimise air space
around the cake.

41

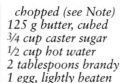

Celebration Cake

Preparation time:
45 minutes
Cooking time:
1¼ hours
Makes one double
20 cm round cake

Dark Layer
¾ cup plain flour
2 tablespoons
 self-raising flour
2 tablespoons cocoa
125 g butter, cubed
125 g dark chocolate,
 chopped
1 cup caster sugar
½ cup hot water
2 teaspoons instant
 coffee powder
2 tablespoons brandy
1 egg, lightly beaten

White Layer
¾ cup plain flour
¼ cup self-raising flour
125 g white chocolate,
 chopped (see Note)
125 g butter, cubed
¾ cup caster sugar
½ cup hot water
2 tablespoons brandy
1 egg, lightly beaten

White Chocolate Cream
125 g white chocolate,
 chopped
1 cup cream, whipped
chocolate curls, for
 decoration

1 Preheat oven to
160°C. Brush two deep
20 cm round cake tins
with melted butter or
oil, line base and sides
with paper; grease paper.
2 To make Dark Layer:
Sift flours and cocoa
into large mixing bowl.
Make a well in the
centre. Place butter,
chocolate, sugar, hot
water and coffee in
basin or top of double
saucepan. Stir over
barely simmering water
until chocolate melts
and the mixture is
smooth; remove from
heat. Cool and stir in
brandy.
3 Add chocolate
mixture and egg to dry
ingredients. Stir with a
wooden spoon until just
combined; do not
overbeat. Pour the
mixture into one of the
prepared tins.
4 To make White
Layer: Sift flours into
large mixing bowl.
Make a well in the
centre. Place chocolate
in basin or top of
double saucepan. Stir
over barely simmering
water until melted;
remove from heat.
Combine butter, sugar
and water in a small
pan. Stir over a low
heat until butter has
melted and sugar
dissolved. Gradually
blend into chocolate.
Cool. Stir in brandy.
Continue as for Step 3.
5 Bake both cakes for
1¼ hours or until
skewer comes out clean
when inserted in centre
of cakes. Stand cakes in
tins 10 minutes before
turning onto wire rack
to cool.
6 To make White
Chocolate Cream: Melt
chocolate as for Step 4.
Cool. Add cream,
beating constantly with
an electric mixer.
7 Sandwich cakes
together with half of the

Celebration Cake.

white chocolate cream.
Cover top and sides of
cake with remainder;
decorate with chocolate
curls (see page 4).

Note: White chocolate
may be difficult to melt,
but white chocolate
buttons will melt more
easily than a block of
chocolate.

Ganache Torte

Preparation time:
  30 minutes
Cooking time:
  20 minutes +
  refrigeration time
Makes 1 x 20 cm round
  torte

Ganache Torte.

1 cup crushed, plain,
  sweet biscuits
100 g pecans, crushed
1 tablespoon brown
  sugar
1 tablespoon coconut
1/4 teaspoon cinnamon
90 g butter, melted

Filling
3/4 cup cream
500 g dark chocolate,
  chopped
1 egg yolk, lightly
  beaten

Sauce
60 g butter
1/2 cup brown sugar
1/3 cup cream

1 Preheat oven to
160°C. Brush a shallow
20 cm flan tin with
melted butter or oil.
2 Combine dry
ingredients in a large
bowl. Add melted
butter. Stir with a
wooden spoon until
well combined. Press
mixture evenly over
base and side of
prepared tin.
3 Bake 20 minutes or
until skewer comes out
clean when inserted in
centre of crust. Stand
crumb crust in tin
5 minutes before turning
onto wire rack to cool.
4 To make Filling:
Place cream in small
pan; bring to boil. Place
chocolate in basin or
top of double saucepan.
Stir over barely
simmering water until
melted; remove from
heat. Cool to room
temperature. Add cream
and egg yolk to the

chocolate. Stir with a
wooden spoon until
well combined. Pour
into prepared crust.
Refrigerate.
5 To make Sauce:
Combine butter and
sugar in a small pan.
Stir over a low heat
until butter has melted
and sugar has dissolved;
remove from heat. Add
cream and stir with a
wooden spoon until
well combined. Cool.
Serve torte in thin
wedges with sauce and
whipped cream.

HINT
Cooking chocolate
has a high
cocoa-butter content.
The flavour is full
and rich. It melts
easily and produces
good results for all
baking purposes.

43

Chocolate Pecan Gateau

Preparation time:
40 minutes
Cooking time:
30 minutes
Makes 1 x 20 cm round cake

1¼ cups self-raising flour
4 tablespoons cocoa
¾ cup brown sugar
¼ cup pecans, chopped
2 eggs, separated
½ cup oil
½ cup milk
½ teaspoon imitation vanilla essence
2 tablespoons rum
½ cup cream, whipped
60 g cooking chocolate, chopped
15 g butter

Mock Cream
125 g butter
1½ cups icing sugar
few drops imitation vanilla essence
1 tablespoon milk
1 tablespoon cocoa
1 tablespoon water

1 Preheat oven to 180°C. Brush two shallow 20 cm round cake tins with melted butter or oil, line base and sides with paper; grease paper.
2 Sift flour and cocoa into large mixer bowl. Stir in sugar and pecans.
3 Pour combined lightly beaten egg yolks, oil, milk and essence onto dry ingredients; beat on low speed for 2 minutes until just moistened.
4 Beat mixture on high speed for 5 minutes or until mixture is free of lumps and increased in volume.
5 Place egg whites in small, clean and dry mixer bowl. Beat until soft peaks form.
6 Using a metal spoon, fold egg whites into mixture quickly and lightly.
7 Pour mixture into prepared tins. Bake 30 minutes or until skewer comes out clean when inserted in centre of cakes. Stand cakes in tins 10 minutes before turning onto wire rack to cool.
8 Cut cakes in half horizontally; drizzle rum over each cut surface. Place first cake layer on a board. Spread cake evenly with cream. Continue layering with remaining cake and

filling, ending with cake on top. Transfer to serving plate.
9 Combine chocolate and butter in a small pan. Stir constantly over low heat until chocolate melts; remove from heat. Spread chocolate evenly over cake, using a warm knife. Allow to set.
10 To make Mock Cream: Beat butter, sugar and essence with electric beaters in small mixer bowl until light and creamy. Gradually add milk, a teaspoon at a time, beating well after each addition. Beat until mixture is smooth and fluffy. Reserve half for decoration.
11 Combine cocoa and water in a small bowl to form a smooth paste. Beat into remaining mock cream. Spread evenly over cake using a spatula dipped in hot water. Pipe an edging around cake rim using the reserved mock cream.

Chocolate Pecan Gateau.

1. For Chocolate Swirl Slice: Press mixture evenly into prepared tin.

2. Place cream cheese, sour cream, eggs, essence and sugar in food-processor bowl.

ingredients into large mixing bowl. Make a well in the centre.
3 Add butter, milk and eggs to dry ingredients. Stir with a wooden spoon until just combined; do not overbeat.
4 Spoon mixture into prepared tin; smooth surface. Bake 25 minutes or until skewer comes out clean when inserted in centre of slice.
5 Stand slice in tin 10 minutes before turning onto wire rack to cool.
6 To make Icing: Combine chocolate and cream in small pan. Stir over low heat until smooth; remove from heat. Cool slightly. Spread evenly over slice using a palette knife. Cut into squares to serve.

HINT
Chocolate is made from the beans of the cacao tree.

Chocolate Swirl Slice

Preparation time:
 30 minutes
Cooking time:
 50 minutes
Makes 1 x 19 cm
 square slice

1 cup plain flour
2 tablespoons custard powder
1/4 cup icing sugar
125 g butter

Filling
250 g cream cheese, chopped
1/4 cup sour cream
2 eggs
1 teaspoon imitation vanilla essence
1/4 cup caster sugar
100 g milk chocolate, chopped

1 Preheat oven to 180°C. Brush a deep 19 cm square cake tin with melted butter or oil, line base and sides with paper; grease paper.
2 Place dry ingredients in food-processor bowl; add butter. Using the pulse action, press button for 15 seconds or until mixture comes together.
3 Press mixture evenly into prepared tin. Bake 15 minutes; remove from oven. Cool for 5 minutes.
4 To make Filling: Place chopped cream cheese, sour cream, eggs, essence and sugar in food-processor bowl. Using the pulse action, process until the mixture is smooth.
5 Place chocolate in glass bowl. Stir over barely simmering water until melted; remove from heat.
6 Pour cream cheese mixture over base. Pour chocolate over mixture at random in a thin stream; swirl with a skewer, making sure not

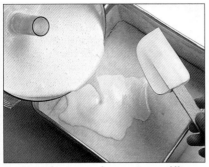

3. *Pour the cream-cheese mixture filling over the base.*

4. *Pour chocolate over mixture in a thin stream; swirl with a skewer.*

to touch the base.
7 Return to oven for 35 minutes or until cream cheese mixture has set. Stand in tin until cool. Cut into squares to serve.

Chocolate and Ricotta Slice

Preparation time:
   25 minutes
Cooking time:
   40-50 minutes
Makes 1 x 23 cm
   square slice

¼ *cup plain flour*
¾ *cup self-raising flour*
¼ *cup cocoa*
½ *cup caster sugar*
1 *egg, lightly beaten*
125 *g butter, melted*
250 *g ricotta cheese*
2 *eggs*
⅓ *cup caster sugar*
2 *tablespoons plain*
   flour
⅓ *cup milk*
1 *tablespoon honey*

1 *teaspoon imitation*
   vanilla essence

1 Preheat oven to 180°C. Brush deep 23 cm square cake tin with melted butter or oil, line base and sides with paper; grease paper.
2 Sift first four ingredients into large mixing bowl. Make a well in the centre.
3 Add egg and butter to dry ingredients. Stir with a wooden spoon until all ingredients are just combined; do not overbeat.
4 Spoon mixture into prepared tin; smooth surface.
5 Place ricotta, eggs, sugar, flour, milk, honey and essence in a food-processor bowl. Using the pulse action, press button for 10 seconds or until mixture is smooth.
6 Pour ricotta mixture over cake base. Bake 50 minutes or until

ricotta mixture has set.
7 Stand slice in tin until cooled. Cut into squares to serve.

Choc Passionfruit Dessert Slice

Preparation time:
   30 minutes
Cooking time:
   Nil
Makes 1 x 20 cm round
   slice

200 *g plain chocolate*
   biscuits, finely crushed
100 *g butter, melted*
⅔ *cup water*
¼ *cup caster sugar*
3 *teaspoons gelatine*
2 *tablespoons*
   passionfruit pulp
50 *g white chocolate,*
   chopped
50 *g dark chocolate,*
   chopped

1 Brush a deep 20 cm springform tin with melted butter or oil.

51

Line base and side with aluminium foil; grease foil.

2 Combine biscuit crumbs and butter, mix well. Press mixture evenly into prepared tin. Refrigerate, covered, until firm.

3 Combine water, sugar and gelatine in a small pan. Stir over low heat until sugar has dissolved. Simmer 5 minutes; remove from heat.

4 Transfer sugar mixture to a medium mixer bowl. Beat on high speed until mixture is white and fluffy. Using a metal spoon, fold in passionfruit. Mix well.

5 Pour passionfruit mixture over base, spread evenly. Refrigerate until set, about 20 minutes.

6 Place white chocolate in glass bowl. Stir over barely simmering water until melted; remove from heat. Repeat for dark chocolate.

7 Pipe chocolate in a loop pattern around the edge of slice. Cut into wedges to serve.

HINT
Cooking times are approximate. They will vary according to the accuracy of the oven temperature and the type of oven.

Choc Rum Slice

Preparation time:
  15 minutes +
  refrigeration time
Cooking time:
  Nil
*Makes 1 x 19 cm
  square slice*

250 g plain chocolate
  biscuits, crushed
1 cup mixed fruit or
  sultanas
1/2 cup walnuts,
  chopped
125 g butter
1/2 cup condensed milk
1 egg
1 teaspoon ground
  cinnamon
2 tablespoons rum
125 g dark chocolate,
  chopped

1 Brush a deep 19 cm square cake tin with melted butter or oil. Line base and sides with aluminium foil; grease foil.

2 Combine biscuit crumbs, fruit and walnuts in large mixing bowl. Make a well in the centre.

3 Combine butter and condensed milk in a small pan. Stir over low heat until butter has melted; remove from heat and whisk in egg, cinnamon and rum.

---

4 Add butter mixture to dry ingredients. Stir with a wooden spoon until well combined.

5 Press mixture evenly into prepared tin.

6 Place chocolate in glass bowl. Stir over barely simmering water until melted; remove from heat.

7 Spread chocolate evenly over slice using a palette knife. Mark into slices. Refrigerate, covered, until it is firm, (see Note). Cut into slices to serve.

Note: Slice will cut better if refrigerated.

HINT
It is possible on occasion to use cocoa instead of chocolate. It still has a good flavour and in some ways is easier to work than chocolate – there's no need for melting, so no risk of scorching! Cocoa is an inexpensive, useful ingredient that you should always have on hand in your larder. Once the packet has been opened, store the contents in an airtight container to retain its freshness.

---

*Choc Passionfruit Dessert Slice
(top, recipe page 51) Choc Rum Slice.*

1. For Date and Chocolate Fudge Slice:
Combine flour, dates, walnuts and rind.

2. Whisk the lightly beaten egg into the
cooled butter mixture.

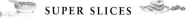

Date and Chocolate Fudge Slice

Preparation time:
 25 minutes
Cooking time:
 25 minutes
Makes one 30 x 20 cm
 oblong slice

1 cup self-raising flour,
 sifted
½ cup dates, chopped
½ cup walnuts,
 chopped
1 teaspoon grated
 lemon rind
125 g butter
1 cup brown sugar
2 tablespoons
 cocoa
2 tablespoons golden
 syrup
1 egg, lightly beaten
60 g dark chocolate,
 chopped

1 Preheat oven to 180°C. Brush a shallow 30 x 20 cm oblong cake tin with melted butter or oil. Cover base with paper extending over two sides; grease paper.
2 Combine flour, dates, walnuts and lemon rind in large mixing bowl. Make a well in the centre.
3 Combine butter, brown sugar, cocoa and golden syrup in a small pan. Stir over low heat until butter has melted and sugar has dissolved; remove from heat. Cool slightly and whisk in the egg.
4 Add butter mixture to dry ingredients. Stir with a metal spoon until well combined.
5 Spoon into prepared tin; smooth surface. Bake 25 minutes or until skewer comes out clean when inserted into centre of slice.

Allow to cool.
6 Place chocolate in glass bowl. Stir over barely simmering water until melted; remove from heat.
7 Drizzle chocolate over slice. Cut into slices to serve.

Sour Cream and Chocolate Slice

Preparation time:
 15 minutes
Cooking time:
 35 minutes
Makes one 30 x 20 cm
 slice

100 g dark chocolate,
 chopped
1 cup caster sugar
1 cup plain flour
¼ cup cocoa
3 eggs
⅔ cup sour cream
150 g butter, melted

Sour Cream and Chocolate Slice (centre), Date and Chocolate Fudge Slice.

3. Add the butter mixture to the dry ingredients. Stir until combined.

4. Spoon the mixture into prepared tin and smooth the top.

Icing
100 g milk chocolate,
  chopped
2 tablespoons sour
  cream

1 Preheat oven to
170°C. Brush a shallow
30 x 20 cm oblong tin
with melted butter or
oil, line base and sides
with paper; grease
paper.
2 Place chocolate in
glass bowl. Stir over
barely simmering water
until melted; remove
from heat.
3 Place all ingredients
into food-processor
bowl. Using the pulse
action, press button for
10 seconds or until
mixture is smooth.
4 Pour mixture into
prepared tin; smooth
surface. Bake for
35 minutes or until
skewer comes out clean
when inserted in centre
of slice.
5 Stand slice in tin 10
minutes before turning
onto wire rack to cool.
6 To make Icing:
Combine chocolate and
sour cream in a small
pan. Stir over low heat
until smooth; remove
from heat. Cool slightly.
Spread evenly over slice
using a palette knife.
Cut into slices to serve.

Chocolate Pecan Slice

Preparation time:
  25 minutes
Cooking time:
  25 minutes
*Makes 1 x 19 cm
  square slice*

1 cup plain flour
1/2 teaspoon
  bicarbonate of soda
1/3 cup ground pecans
1/4 cup caster sugar
90 g butter
1/4 cup golden syrup
100 g dark chocolate,
  chopped
2 eggs, lightly beaten

Icing
100 g dark chocolate,
  chopped
1/4 cup sour cream
whole pecans

1 Preheat oven to
180°C. Brush a shallow
19 cm square cake tin
with melted butter or
oil, line base and sides
with paper; grease
paper.
2 Sift first four
ingredients into large
mixing bowl. Make a
well in the centre.
3 Combine butter,
syrup and chocolate in
a small pan. Stir over
low heat until mixture
is smooth. Remove
from heat; whisk in
the eggs.
4 Add butter mixture

to dry ingredients. Stir
with a wooden spoon
until just combined; do
not overbeat.
5 Pour mixture into
prepared tin. Bake
25 minutes or until
skewer comes out clean
when inserted in centre
of slice.
6 Stand slice in tin 10
minutes before turning
onto wire rack to cool.
7 To make Icing:
Combine chocolate
and sour cream in a
small pan. Stir over low
heat until smooth;
remove from heat. Cool
slightly. Spread evenly
over slice using a
palette knife; top with
whole pecans. Cut into
slices to serve.

Choc Honeycomb Slice

Preparation time:
  20 minutes
Cooking time:
  25 minutes
*Makes 1 x 19 cm
  square slice*

125 g butter
1/3 cup caster sugar
2 eggs
100 g chocolate-coated
  honeycomb, crumbled
2/3 cup plain flour, sifted
1/3 cup self-raising flour,
  sifted
1 tablespoon cocoa,
  sifted
1/4 cup milk

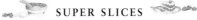

Choc Honeycomb Slice (left), Chocolate Pecan Slice.

Icing
50 g chocolate, chopped
100 g cream cheese
2 teaspoons honey

1 Preheat oven to 180°C. Brush a deep 19 cm square cake tin with melted butter or oil, line base and sides with paper; grease paper.

2 Beat butter and sugar with electric beaters in small mixer bowl until light and creamy. Add eggs gradually, beating well after each addition.

3 Transfer mixture to large mixing bowl; add honeycomb. Using a metal spoon, fold in sifted ingredients alternately with milk. Stir until just combined and the mixture is almost smooth.

4 Spoon mixture into prepared tin; smooth surface. Bake 25 minutes or until skewer comes out clean when inserted in centre of the slice.

5 Stand slice in tin 10 minutes before turning onto wire rack to cool.

6 To make Icing: Place chocolate in glass bowl. Stir over barely simmering water until melted; remove from heat.

7 Beat cream cheese and honey with electric beaters in small mixer bowl until creamy. Add chocolate, beat until combined and smooth. Spread evenly over slice using a palette knife. Serve cut into squares.

3 Combine condensed milk, butter and chocolate in large pan. Stir over low heat until mixture is smooth. Add nuts, stir until combined.

4 Pour nut mixture over base, spread evenly. Refrigerate until set, about 20 minutes. Cut into bars to serve.

Note: Any combination of nuts or dried fruits to a quantity of 1¼ cups can be used.

Nutty Chocolate Slice

Preparation time:
  20 minutes
Cooking time:
  25 minutes
Makes 1 x 19 cm
  square slice

100 g butter
¼ cup caster sugar
1 egg, lightly beaten
1 teaspoon imitation
  vanilla essence
1 cup self-raising flour,
  sifted
1 tablespoon cocoa,
  sifted
1 tablespoon drinking
  chocolate, sifted
½ cup condensed milk
½ cup brown sugar
⅓ cup crushed nuts

1 Preheat oven to 180°C. Brush a deep 19 cm square cake tin

with melted butter or oil, line base and sides with paper; grease paper.

2 Beat butter and sugar with electric beaters in small mixer bowl until light and creamy. Add egg and essence; beat until combined.

3 Transfer mixture to medium mixing bowl. Using a metal spoon, fold in sifted flour, cocoa and drinking chocolate. Stir until combined.

4 Spread mixture evenly into prepared tin.

5 Combine condensed milk, brown sugar and nuts in small mixing bowl. Stir until combined; pour over base mixture in tin. Bake 25 minutes or until skewer comes out clean when inserted in centre of slice.

6 Stand slice in tin 10 minutes before turning onto wire rack to cool. Serve cut into squares.

> ### HINT
> The South American Aztec Indians were believed to be the first people in the world to drink chocolate – they used it as a stimulant. Its popularity gradually spread worldwide after Spanish explorers brought it to Europe in the sixteenth century.

Chocolate and Toffee Slice

Preparation time:
  30 minutes
Cooking time:
  25 minutes
Makes 1 x 19 cm
  square slice

1 cup self-raising flour
¼ cup cocoa
½ cup caster sugar
125 g butter, melted

Caramel
1 teaspoon butter
1 tablespoon golden
  syrup
½ cup condensed milk

Toffee
½ cup caster sugar
75 g walnuts, chopped

1 Preheat oven to 180°C. Brush a deep 19 cm square cake tin with melted butter or oil, line base and sides with paper; grease paper.

2 Sift the flour and cocoa into bowl. Stir in the sugar. Make a well in the centre, stir in the butter until all the ingredients are well combined.

3 Press mixture into prepared tin; smooth surface. Bake 25 minutes or until skewer comes out clean when inserted in centre of slice.

4 Stand slice in tin 10 minutes before turning

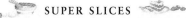

onto wire rack to cool.
5 To make Caramel:
Combine butter, syrup
and condensed milk in
a small pan. Stir over
low heat until smooth;
remove from heat. Cool
slightly. Spread evenly
over slice using a
palette knife.
6 To make Toffee:
Dissolve sugar in a
small pan over low heat
until golden in colour;
remove from heat. Stir
in nuts. Pour mixture
onto foil-covered tray.
Allow to set. Peel off
foil, place in plastic bag
and crush with a rolling
pin. Sprinkle over slice.
Serve cut in slices.

Chocolate Coconut Delight.

Chocolate Coconut Delight

Preparation time:
  20 minutes
Cooking time:
  20 minutes
*Makes one 30 x 20 cm
  slice*

1¾ *cups self-raising
  flour*
2 *tablespoons cocoa*
1 *cup desiccated
  coconut*
½ *cup caster sugar*
½ *cup walnuts,
  chopped*
180 g *butter*
1 *teaspoon imitation
  vanilla essence*
1 *tablespoon golden
  syrup*

Chocolate Icing
2 *cups icing sugar, sifted*
2 *tablespoons cocoa,
  sifted*
1 *teaspoon imitation
  vanilla essence*
30 g *butter*
2-3 *tablespoons hot
  water*

1 Preheat oven to
180°C. Brush a shallow
30 x 20 cm oblong cake
tin with melted butter
or oil. Cover base and
sides with paper,
extending over two
sides; grease paper.
2 Sift flour and cocoa
into large mixing bowl.
Add coconut, sugar and
walnuts. Make a well in
the centre.
3 Combine butter,

essence and golden
syrup in a small pan.
Stir over low heat until
butter has melted;
remove from heat.
4 Add butter mixture
to sifted ingredients.
Stir with a wooden
spoon until ingredients
are well combined.
5 Press mixture evenly
into prepared tin. Bake
20 minutes or until
skewer comes out clean
when inserted into
centre of slice.
6 To make Chocolate
Icing: Combine all
ingredients. Mix well
until smooth. Spread
evenly over cool slice
using a palette knife.
Cut slice into squares
to serve.

Chocolate Muesli Slice

Preparation time:
  15 minutes
Cooking time:
  25 minutes
Makes 1 x 19 cm
  square slice

3/4 cup toasted muesli
1 cup self-raising flour,
  sifted
2 tablespoons cocoa,
  sifted
125 g butter
1 tablespoon golden
  syrup
1/2 cup brown sugar
2 eggs, lightly beaten
1/4 cup milk
60 g chocolate, chopped

1 Preheat oven to
180°C. Brush a deep
19 cm square cake tin
with melted butter or
oil, line base and sides
with paper; grease paper.
2 Combine muesli,
sifted flour and cocoa in
a large mixing bowl.
Make a well in the centre.
3 Combine butter,
golden syrup and
brown sugar in a small
pan. Stir over low heat
until butter has melted
and sugar has dissolved;
remove from heat.
4 Add butter mixture,
eggs and milk to dry
ingredients. Stir with a
wooden spoon until the
ingredients are just
combined; do not

overbeat the mixture.
5 Pour mixture into
prepared tin; smooth
surface. Bake 25 minutes
or until skewer comes
out clean when inserted
in centre of cake.
6 Stand slice in tin
for 6 minutes before
turning onto wire rack
to cool.
7 Place chocolate in
glass bowl. Stir over
barely simmering water
until melted; remove
from heat.
8 Drizzle chocolate
onto slice. Cut into
squares to serve.

Fruity Chocolate Slice

Preparation time:
  20 minutes
Cooking time:
  Nil
Makes one 30 x 20 cm
  slice

1 x 250 g plain sweet
  biscuits, crushed
1 cup bottled fruit
  mince (mincemeat)
1/4 cup almonds,
  chopped
2 tablespoons brandy
100 g butter
100 g dark chocolate,
  chopped

Icing
1 tablespoon cocoa,
  sifted

1/4 cup icing sugar, sifted
1 tablespoon warm
  water
30 g unsalted butter,
  softened
desiccated coconut, to
  garnish

1 Brush a shallow
30 x 20 cm oblong cake
tin with melted butter
or oil. Line base and
sides with aluminium
foil; grease foil.
2 Combine biscuits,
fruit mince, almonds
and brandy in large
mixing bowl. Make a
well in the centre.
3 Combine butter and
chocolate in glass bowl.
Stir over barely
simmering water until
melted; remove from
heat.
4 Add chocolate
mixture to biscuit
mixture. Stir with a
wooden spoon until
well combined.
5 Press mixture evenly
into prepared tin.
Refrigerate, covered,
until firm.
6 To make Icing:
Combine cocoa, icing
sugar and water in a
small bowl, stir until
smooth. Whisk in
softened butter. Spread
icing evenly over slice
using a palette knife.
7 Sprinkle with coconut
and leave to set. Cut into
slices and store, covered,
in the refrigerator.

Left: Fruity Chocolate Slice, Chocolate Muesli Slice.

Index